IMAGES OF ENGLAND

# WORKINGTON

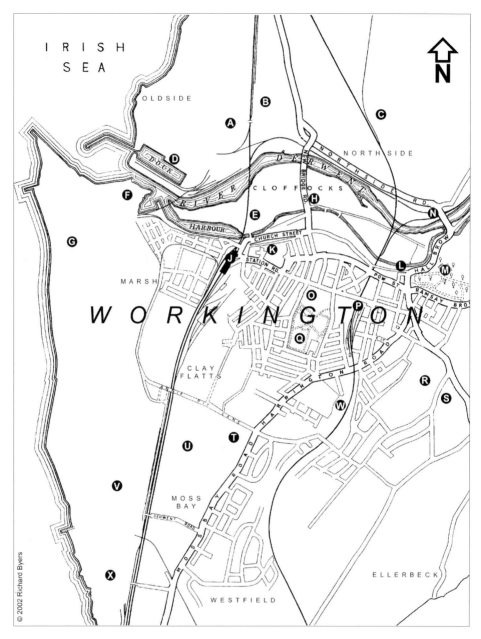

Map of the town of Workington, *c.* 1950. To assist the reader many of the most significant buildings and sites mentioned in this book are identified on this plan. (A) Workington Haematite Ironworks. (B) West Cumberland Haematite Ironworks. (C) Burrow Walls Roman Camp. (D) Prince of Wales Dock. (E) Derwent Park. (F) Shipyards. (G) How Michael. (H) Borough Park. (J) Low Station. (K) St Michael's Parish Church. (L) High Brewery M) Workington Hall. (N) Bridge Station. (O) Technical College. (P) Central Station. (Q) Vulcans Park. (R) Bankfield Mansion. (S) Newlands School. (T) Jane Pit. (U) Solway Colliery. (V) Charles Cammell Iron & Steelworks. (W) Workington Infirmary. (X) Moss Bay Iron & Steelworks.

IMAGES OF ENGLAND

# WORKINGTON

RICHARD L.M. BYERS

TEMPUS

First published 2004

Tempus Publishing Limited
The Mill, Brimscombe Port,
Stroud, Gloucestershire, GL5 2QG
www.tempus-publishing.com

British Library Cataloguing in Publication Data.
A catalogue record for this book is available from the British Library.

ISBN 0 7524 3295 8
Typesetting and origination by Tempus Publishing Limited.
Printed in Great Britain.

# Contents

# Acknowledgements

I wish to acknowledge the ready help and assistance given to me by so many who directly or indirectly contributed to this book. My special thanks are due to Jo Byers, Michael Burridge, Janet Thompson, Ray Richardson, Andy Byers, Joyce Byers, Philip Crouch (Helena Thompson Museum), the Bessemer Steel Archive, Workington Public Library, Whitehaven and Carlisle Record Offices.

A photograph looking east from the railway station directly up Station Road, towards St Michael's school in the distance. The elaborate floral arch spanning across this busy street was built to celebrate the coronation of Edward VII in 1902. The new king was the eldest son of Queen Victoria and Prince Albert. To the right of the picture is the Commercial Hotel, now the Cumberland Hotel (see page 22), whilst to the left are the premises of Joseph Huntrods & Co., ships chandlers, ironmongers and mill furnishers. Joseph Huntrods (1852-1923), who was also the chairman of the Workington Bridge and Boiler Co., founded this business in 1873. In addition to his business activities he also had a passion for rugby league, and was appointed the first president of the Cumberland County Rugby Football League, serving till 1901.

# Introduction

My primary objective in compiling this collection of archive images of Workington is to bring together some of the most important photographs and much of the previously unpublished material I had unearthed during my research. I have endeavoured to arranged them in order to provide a concise visual history of this prominent West Cumbrian town. Many of these fascinating images will no doubt provide those who have grown up in this area with a nostalgic look back to times past and an opportunity to reflect on how things have changed.

Workington's long history can be traced back to at least the second century with the evidence of a Roman station at Burrow Walls. This fort known as Gabrosentum is believed to have been an integral part of the coastal defences that are known to have once extended south from the western end of Hadrian's Wall. A basic analysis of the place name suggests that an Anglo-Saxon settlement with a chief called Weorc or Wyrc was later established here, close to the mouth of the River Derwent. Other significant Anglo-Saxon and Viking evidence has also been unearthed in the town to confirm this, principally in and around the ancient parish church of St Michael. From the designs on carved stone fragments we can now plot the towns history up to the time of William the Conqueror.

Upon the site of Burrow Walls was built a Norman castle, some remains of which can still be seen. This was erected by the forebears of the influential Curwen family who were Lords of the Manor of Workington for almost eight hundred years. Later, around 1250, they moved their home south across the River Derwent and built a fortified pele tower to resist the marauding Border Reivers. Parts of this substantial structure can still be identified within the ruins of Workington Hall. Mary Queen of Scots famously rested here in May 1568 spending her last night of freedom in the town, before being arrested and implicated in a plot to murder her cousin, Elizabeth I. In Georgian times, the Hall was greatly extended and remodelled into the large and elegant mansion house which played host to many prominent visitors, including William and Dorothy Wordsworth.

From the early eighteenth century Workington survived and prospered by virtue of its rich coal deposits, which were mined extensively and shipped out of its growing port. Shipbuilding was also a significant industry, employing several generations of the townspeople. A century later the town became a major centre for the production of iron and steel. During the 1870s and '80s, Workington's population almost doubled. Row upon row of small terraced houses were built to accommodate the influx of these workers and their families. Victorian Workington grew dramatically, but was very much different than today. For instance, the numerous small independent shops and businesses have almost disappeared. Entire communities have been cleared and rehoused and when the town centre was last redeveloped in the late 1960s many of its older streets and buildings were lost forever.

*Richard Byers*
*August 2004*

William Carruthers Lawrie's photograph looking east along a busy Pow Street, from its junction with John Street, *c.* 1910. To the right of the picture is Henry McAleer's boot and shoe shop, which once boasted it had over 4,000 pairs of shoes in stock. Prices then varied from 4/9 to 15/6. These premises were built on the site of a large house once occupied by Thomas Iredale who established the Workington Brewery Company. The Griffin Hotel and the local branch of the Bank of Whitehaven can be seen in the distance on the left-hand side of the road. The Bank of Whitehaven, which was established in 1837, was taken over by the Manchester and Liverpool District Bank in 1916. Around eight years later its name was shortened and it became known as the District Bank.

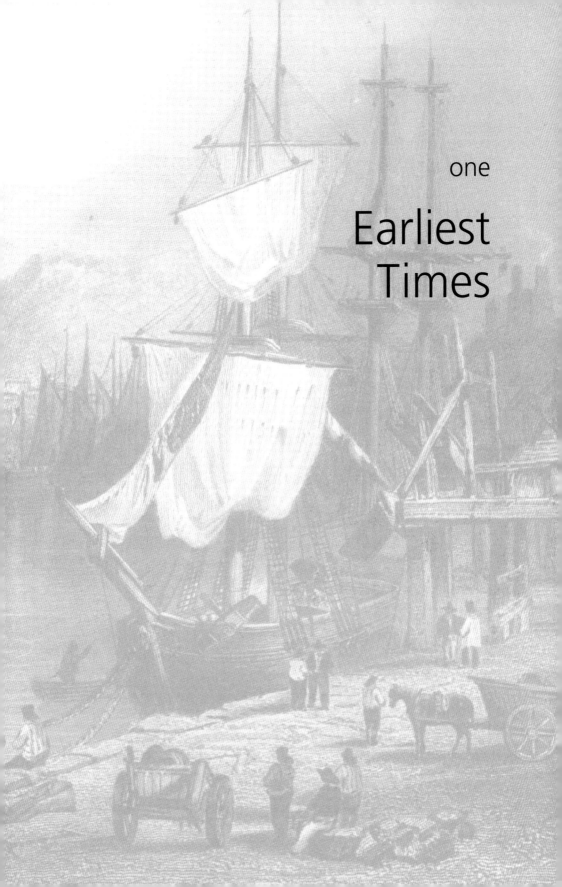

one

# Earliest
# Times

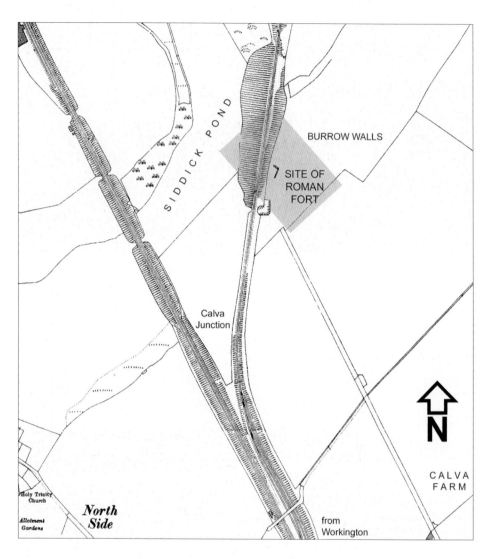

Plan showing the location of Gabrosentum, the Roman fort at Burrow Walls, based on the 1923 Ordnance Survey map. The site is identified on the location plan at the beginning of this book (see p. 2) by the letter C. The shaded area shows the approximate extent of the fort, which is believed to have measured 88.4m (290ft) across its ramparts and be some 137.2m (450ft) in length. However, the latter dimension is only an estimate as the western portion of the fort appears to have been lost due to erosion of the cliff face above Siddick Pond. A good section of this is also buried below the old railway embankment which crosses the site. The L-shaped existing walls of the old Norman tower are also indicated.

A view of the 1955 excavations at Burrow Walls, looking north west with the spoil heap and pithead of St Helen's colliery in the distance. For many years some of the most eminent Roman historians and archaeologists overlooked and dismissed the site as quite insignificant. However, Richard Bellhouse, Iain McIvor and Brian Blake carried out a well planned and professional investigation confirming for the first time the existence and the extent of the second-century Roman fort.

A further photograph of the 1955 excavations on the site of the Roman camp at Burrow Walls (Northside), this time looking almost due west. The old Cumberland Cloth Factory can be seen to the right, on the site presently occupied by the Dunmail Park retail complex. The railway embankment along the edge of Siddick Pond runs left to right and the stonework remains of the eleventh-century fort can be seen in the centre of the picture.

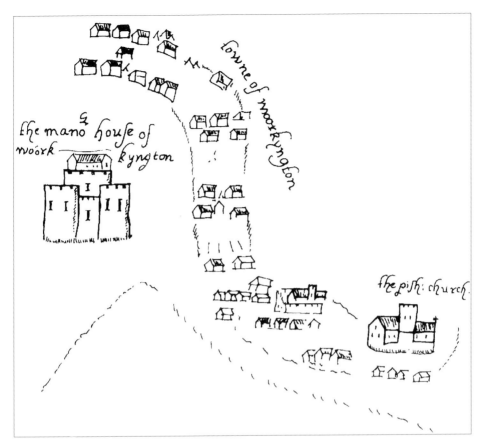

The mano house of woork — kyngton

towne of woorkyngton

the p'sh: church.

The earliest surviving plan of the town was produced in 1569, less than twelve months after the visit of Mary Queen of Scots. Workington Hall to the left and St Michael's parish church to the right are the most prominent properties. The road linking the two appears to follow the line of what we know today as Brow Top and Church Street. There appear to be no more than thirty or so other dwellings, suggesting the town's population at this time was little more than a few hundred.

*Opposite:* Sketch of some of the carved stones found at St Michael's church, which provide a valuable insight into the early history of the town. The markings on the stones to the bottom right and top right are thought to be Anglo-Saxon dating from the eighth or ninth century. Whilst the remainder show significant Scandinavian or Viking influence and date from the mid-tenth century. The designs on these stones are often dismissed as simple decoration, but it is thought by many that they were not purely for ornamentation. There is believed to be a code to these patterns, a meaning or significance perhaps Christian or maybe political. No one has yet positively deciphered their message. Of particular significance is the inter-laced stranded plait-work design on the stone to the bottom centre. This appears to have been influenced by the similar fret-work patterns on the Curwen family coat of arms. We certainly know from other sources that the early ancestors of the Curwen family had held the manor of Workington since the early years of the eleventh century.

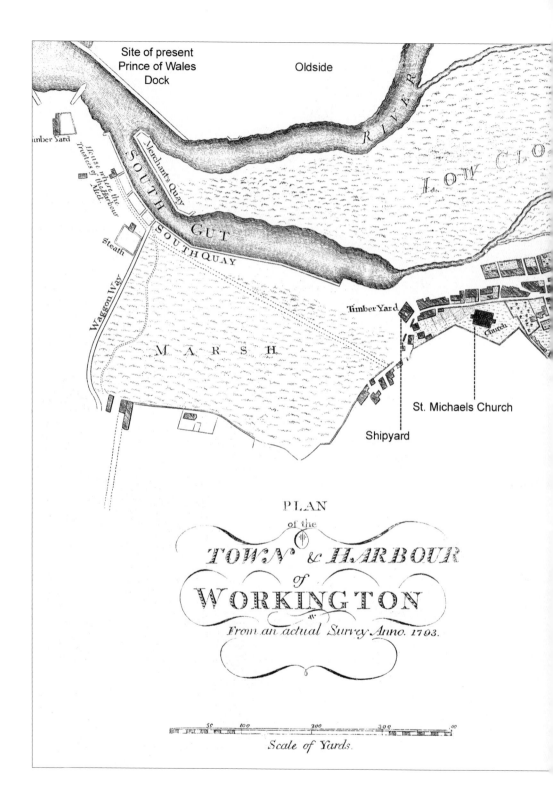

Site of present
Prince of Wales
Dock

Oldside

RIVER

LOW CLO

Timber Yard

House where the
Trustees of the Harbour
Med.

Merchant's Quay

SOUTH

GUT

SOUTH QUAY

Steath

Waggon Way

MARSH

Timber Yard

Church

St. Michaels Church

Shipyard

PLAN
of the
TOWN & HARBOUR
of
WORKINGTON
From an actual Survey Anno. 1793.

50   100      200      300      400

Scale of Yards.

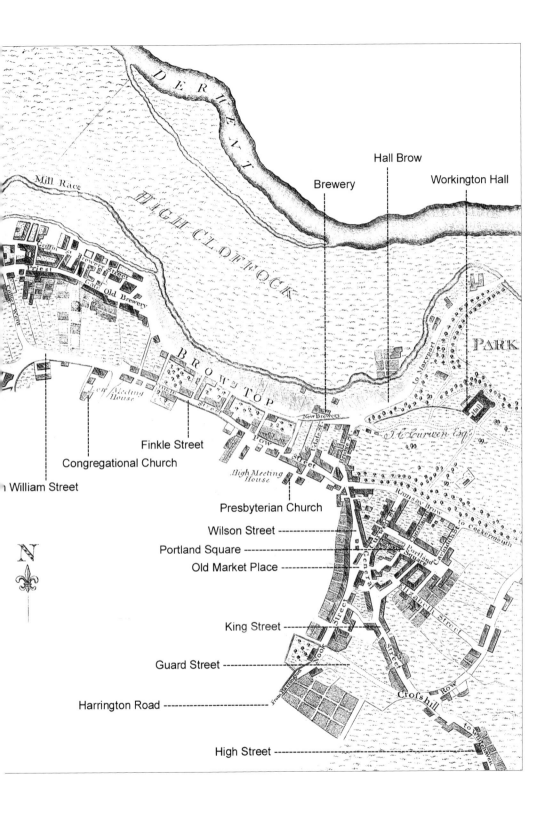

Hall Brow

Brewery

Workington Hall

Mill Race

DERWENT

HIGH CLOSE OCK

BROW TOP

PARK

Old Brewery

New Brewery

J.C. Curwen Esq.

Hall

Low Meeting House

Finkle Street

Congregational Church

High Meeting House

William Street

Ramsey Brow

to Cockermouth

Presbyterian Church

Wilson Street - - - - - - - - -

Portland Square - - - - - - - - -

Old Market Place - - - - - - - -

Portland Square

N

King Street - - - - - - - -

Guard Street - - - - - - - - - -

Crofs hill Row

Harrington Road - - - - - - - - - - - - - - - >

High Street - - - - - - - - - -

RIVER DERWENT

SAND BANK

EARLY QUAYSIDE

OLD LINE OF RIVER

CLOFFOLKS

*Previous pages:* A plan of the town and harbour of Workington, based on a 1793 map commissioned by John Christian Curwen for inclusion in Hutchinson's *History of Cumberland.* Workington at the end of the eighteenth century was quite different to the Workington of today, there was no Washington Street or any other roads south of Pow Street. Brow Top was still the main thoroughfare between the top of the town and the harbour area. In order that the old plan may be more easily understood, additional notes have been added to identify various streets and buildings that still exist today.

ST MICHAELS CHURCH

SHIP YARD

WORKINGTON HALL

PRIESTGATE MARSH

*These pages:* Joseph Farington's steel engraving of Workington looking from the south west. This print published in Lyson's *Magna Britannia* is dated 1815. However, the artist may well have sketched the scene many years earlier as construction work to Workington Hall, on the centre of the right-hand page, is clearly not yet complete. Of further interest is the course of the River Derwent which was then quite different from today. Before the construction of Merchants Quay, part of the river actually curved south and would have flowed alongside the South Quay.

One of the few surviving photographs of the Elizabethan chapel known as How Michael, which once stood on the summit of the shoreline cliffs above Clay Flatts. William Whelan in 1860 described the almost square two-storey building as having an arched ground floor and 'a narrow winding staircase, sufficient for the passage of one person' leading up to the top floor. There are few surviving records to provide us with any real information about the chapel, but its location and fortified appearance suggest it may have also served as a watch tower, during the time of the English and Scottish border feuding. We also know that it was once kept 'regularly whitewashed' to act as a prominent landmark guiding mariners along the Solway Firth.

*Previous page:* William H. Bartlett's finely detailed 1837 steel engraving of Workington harbour, viewed from the west and looking along the South Gut towards St Michael's church in the distance. Of particular interest are the coal hurries to the right on the South Quay. The wagons of coal were drawn up an incline onto these raised timber structures allowing them to be easily and quickly emptied into the hold of the waiting sailing ships. This system was designed to decrease loading time and speedily turn the ships around.

# two

# Old
# Workington

A view looking west down Station Road towards the LNWR railway station, *c.* 1910. The junction with Dean Street can be seen to the right of the picture. Although many of these original buildings still remain, the street is now almost totally devoid of any shops. It was once one of the principle shopping streets in the town. Today, the majority of its Victorian shopfronts have been removed and the properties converted to other uses.

The Commercial Hotel on the corner of Station Road and Belle Isle Street, viewed from the entrance to the railway station opposite. Built in the 1870s by the Iredale Bros who ran the High Brewery in Ladies Walk, the hotel was eventually acquired by the Workington Brewery Co. Attached to the hotel was a dwelling house, a cottage and five office suites. One of these served as the headquarters of the Cleator and Workington Junction Railway Co., until the extensions to Central Station were completed. During the 1960s, the Commercial Hotel changed its name to the Cumberland Arms Hotel.

A photograph of the once busy shops on the south side of Station Road viewed from the junction with Hagg Hill, c. 1903. Upwards of five hundred new terraced houses were built in this part of the town around 1890 and Station Road developed into a flourishing shopping street. On the far corner of Lonsdale Street, to the right of the picture is the No. 1 branch of the Workington and District Industrial and Provident Co-operative Society, opened in 1897. To the far left is the grocers shop belonging to Joseph Goss, who had three other shops in the town. These were located on Pow Street, Harrington Road and Moss Bay Road. When the shop eventually closed in the 1970s, it is believed some of the antiquated old shopfittings were acquired by the Beamish museum in the north east.

A photograph of a busy Hagg Hill (or Falcon Place) on market day, viewed from Station Road, c. 1912. Although the town's market charter dates back to the sixteenth century, regular markets were only held here from around the mid-1880s. On the far right is the entrance to Whitfields Arcade. Part of this building opened in May 1886, served as a market hall with a number of permanent stallholders. It also contained a large public hall, much of which eventually became the Hippodrome cinema. The large building in the centre of the picture is Dent Hall at the bottom of Fisher Street.

A 1923 view of a very busy Fisher Street, looking east from its junction with North Watts Street. Like Station Road this was once one of the most prominent shopping streets in the town. The end of Duke Street can be seen in the centre of the photograph, and the block just past this junction contained a large public hall, known as the Albert Hall.

The Workington Beehive Co-operative Society premises on the west side of Vulcans Lane, c. 1934. Today the site opposite the bus station is occupied by Simon House. This co-operative society was formed in 1884, principally by a group of employees of the Charles Cammell Iron and Steel works. The society expanded rapidly and by 1924 had over 4,200 members and annual sales of over £116,000. They also operated branches at Napier Street, Southey Street, Harrington Road, Senhouse Street, Westfield, Siddick, Bridgefoot, Harrington and Seaton.

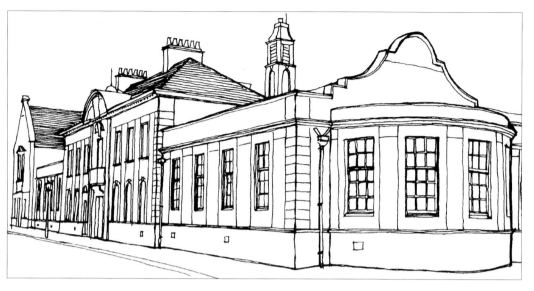

Sketch of the Carnegie public library and lecture hall building on the east corner of Finkle Street and Vulcans Lane. Like many other municipal projects of the time, several architects were invited to submit their designs for the new building. The open competition attracted seventy-four entries and the winners were Messrs W.A. Mellon and George Wittet (of York). Alderman R.E. Highton formally laid the foundation stone for the new library on 10 September 1903. The contractor for the red sandstone building was Messrs J.I. Wilson and Co.

The Council Chamber at the Carnegie Library, used from around 1907 by the Borough Council for its meetings. This large room was located at the front of the building, immediately to the left of the front entrance into the library. The walls were adorned with large portraits of the town's former mayors, those above include Henry Fraser Curwen and James Duffield.

*Above:* The entrance foyer of the former Carnegie public library in Finkle Street, opened in October 1904. Funded by the philanthropist Andrew Carnegie, the town's first purpose-built library cost nearly £7,000, with the site being provided free by the Borough Council. The process of borrowing a book was quite different to today. All books for 'lending' were kept behind the counter and borrowers had to request the title from the assistant.

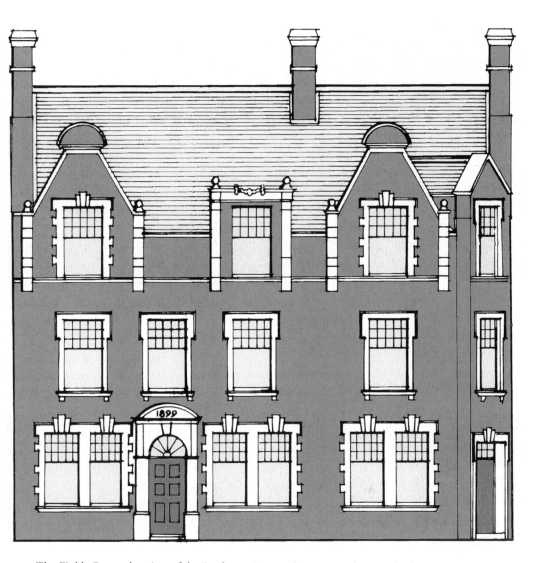

The Finkle Street elevation of the Appletree Inn, on the corner of Warwick Place and Finkle Street, based on the original architects drawings. Although owned by the Workington Brewery Co., the cost of building this public house in 1899 was actually funded by the Borough Council. They agreed to pay for the new building, in order that that an older pub of the same name could be demolished to make way for the widening of Finkle Street.

*Opposite below:* The interior of Workington Public Library in the 1930s when it was housed in the Carnegie building on Finkle Street. By this time the antiquated method of borrowers requesting books over a counter had been superceded by the open shelf system. Readers could now freely browse through the titles available in a new more relaxed environment, albeit in strict silence.

An early photograph of Finkle Street looking towards the Wesleyan Methodist church, *c.* 1890. Originally, this busy street was much narrower than today. Along its south side were a row of about eight small whitewashed cottages built in 1728 by the Curwen family. In January 1894, when work began to widen Finkle Street, these properties were the first to be demolished.

Lister's Derwent Furnishing House on the north side of Finkle Street is one of the oldest surviving businesses in the town and still trades today from premises further up the same street. Built in 1901, this large shop extended back into Derwent House in Brow Top, the former home of shipbuilder James Alexander (1799-1881). To the left of the photograph are the remains of the old cottages on the south side of Finkle Street. These were eventually demolished along with the old Appletree Inn in order to widen the street.

The former post office building on the corner of Murray Road and Finkle Street, *c.* 1929. This substantial red sandstone and brick building replaced the earlier post office in John Street. Up until at least the 1960s, all the town's mail was sorted and despatched from these premises. The tower of the Wesleyan Methodist church can be seen in the distance at the opposite end of Finkle Street. The attractive facade of the former Lister's store is on the far right of the picture.

Almost the same view along Finkle Street, during the early 1960s. While the last photograph was totally devoid of any motor cars, the street here (like today) is very congested. But there is now one obvious major difference, vehicles are thankfully no longer allowed to pass in both directions. To the right, Simmons Furnishers now occupy Lister's old shop and the front of the premises has been modernised. However, a close look at the building today still reveals some of its old Victorian features.

A 1944 photograph of the Signal Section of the Headquarter Company of the Workington Home Guard, pictured outside Tuscan Villa in South William Street. Their main function was to maintain communications in the event of an invasion or other emergency. Left to right, back row: Pte A. McMullen, Pte R. Fishwick, Pte J. Edwards, Pte J. Hunter, Cpl W. Cockton. Middle row: Pte H. Boswell, Pte T.H. Cowan, Pte R. Simpson, Pte S. Ray, Pte R. McNarry, Pte A. Byers, Pte J. Watchorne. Front row: Pte B. Needham, Cpl S. Price, Lt J. Mounsey, Capt F. Gregory, Lt T. Fletcher, Sgt A. Banks, L/Cpl J. Bacon, T. Mitchell (Black Watch).

The Mayors of Workington (Councillor Lancaster) and Whitehaven (Councillor Harrison) accompanied by Col T. Dix-Perkin, Sub-District Commander begin their march to the Saluting Base during the Stand Down Parade of the Workington Home Guard on 3 December 1944. This was located at the junction of Murray Road and Oxford Street, outside the bus station. They are flanked on either side by a guard of honour made up of members of A Company, formed from men employed at the Workington Iron and Steel Co.

Col T. Dix-Perkin, Sub-District Commander inspects the Guard of Honour assembled outside the Carnegie Library in Finkle Street. The town's Local Defence Volunteers, formed in 1940, were affiliated to the Border Regiment and known as the 5th (Cumberland) Battalion Home Guard.

Despite the Stand Down Parade of the Workington Home Guard taking place in a violent rainstorm, the route was lined by many local people who had come to pay tribute to their citizen soldiers. This photograph, looking east along Oxford Street, records the Drums of the 5th (Cumb.) Battalion passing the Saluting Base, outside the bus station. The band then played past the remaining members of the Battalion, which numbered nearly 4,000 volunteers.

POW STREET. WORKINGTON.

The splendid 1920s interior of the Midland Bank (now HSBC) at the east end of Pow Street. These bank premises had originally been built for the Cumberland Union Bank in 1865. Through a series of amalgamations the Midland acquired control of the locally based bank and subsequently changed its name. One feature of the highly-polished mahogany counter was the series of brass light fittings which were a common feature of the many new Midland Bank interiors around the time of the First World War.

*Opposite above:* A 1950s view of Pow Street, looking west towards Finkle Street. To the left is the end of John Street, which originally crossed over Central Square and continued all the way through to Pow Street. This section of the street disappeared with the building of St John's shopping precinct in the late 1960s. The block of property on the left which included Goss' grocers shop, the Grapes Inn public house, Timpsons shoe shop and W.H. Smith's store was also demolished during this redevelopment.

*Opposite below:* Looking east along Pow Street from its junction with John Street, in the opposite direction to the previous picture, *c.* 1914. The Griffin Hotel can be seen in the distance and John Mandale's clock and watchmakers is on the right, beneath the large circular projecting clock. Of particular interest are the row of very large electric arc lights at the entrance to the Jubilee Opera House on the immediate left. Installed in 1911, these were powered by a private generator as an electricity supply was not available in the town until 1925.

Hattersley's boot and shoe shop on the corner of Pow Street and Washington Street, next to the former Cumberland Union Bank, *c.* 1910. This extensive business was established by John Henry Hattersley, the son of a Glossop cobbler who married a Workington girl. It is though that the gentleman pictured in the doorway of the shop is J.H. Hattersley, while the young man is his son Albert Henry, who later ran a similar shop in Station Road during the 1930s.

A view of Pow Street, looking west from its junction with Washington Street. Hattersley's boot and shoe shop is on the immediate left, while the block of property opposite on the right, which once included the Pineapple public house, today forms part of the car park in front of present Marks & Spencer store. It was at this end of the street that the famous travelling street musician, Jimmy Dyer, is said to have regularly performed.

A photograph looking north along Washington Street towards the end of Pow Street, c. 1915. If we think about this wide busy street today, it is difficult to imagine that there was once shops on the north side of Pow Street, extended across the end of Washington Street to the bottom of Wilson Street and Ramsey Brow. In order to reach Hall Brow, vehicles passing along Washington Street had to make a very tight right turn and then a left into Bridge Street (see aerial photograph on following page).

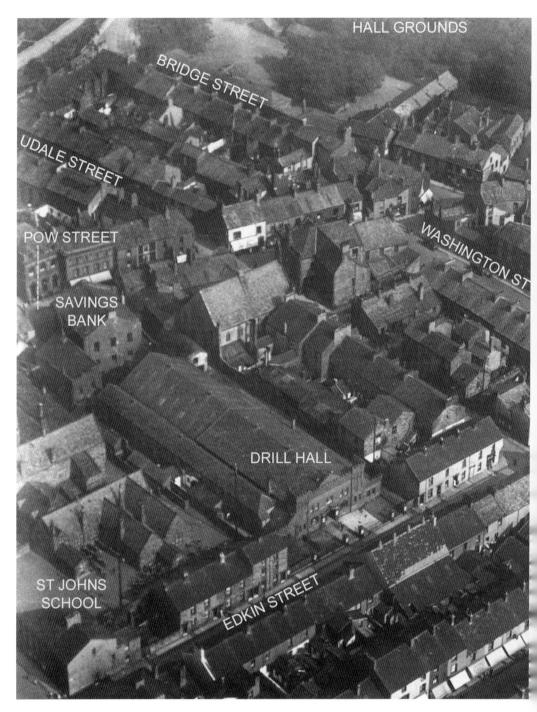

HALL GROUNDS

BRIDGE STREET

UDALE STREET

POW STREET

SAVINGS BANK

WASHINGTON ST

DRILL HALL

ST JOHNS SCHOOL

EDKIN STREET

A 1929 aerial photograph of the properties immediately west of Washington Street, cleared in the late 1960s and '70s to make way for the town centre redevelopment. In the centre of the picture is the Drill Hall in Edkin Street (see p. 37) and at its rear, facing onto Pow Street, was the old Savings Bank building. The upper section of John Street running from Central Square to Pow Street crosses the bottom left, and here was St John's School (see p. 112).

The Artillery Drill Hall, on the north side of Edkin Street. Edkin Street ran parallel with Jane Street between Washington Street and the upper section of John Street. During the late 1960s, the entire street was cleared to make way for the town centre redevelopment. The Drill Hall was built in 1900-01 and located behind St John's School and extended to the rear of the old Savings Bank building in Pow Street. A key feature of the building was its finely detailed red brickwork façade.

An early photograph of Portland Square in Victorian times, viewed from the south east. In the top right-hand corner of this picturesque cobbled square were the old Assembly Rooms. The L-shaped building was often used for public meetings, dinners and balls. It also played host to a number of important visitors , including Oscar Wilde who delivered a lecture there in 1884. The tall grey marble obelisk in the centre of the square was erected as a memorial to Dr Anthony Peat who died in June 1877.

A view of the corner of Bridge Street and Udale Street, looking south west from the top of Hall Brow, shortly before its demolition in the 1970s. The Globe Inn had existed here from at least 1834, when the landlord was William Iredale. The public house was later acquired by the Workington Brewery Co., whose brewery was just across the street in Ladies Walk.

A 1970s view looking north along Bridge Street, towards the top of Hall Brow. This street has now virtually disappeared from Workington's street map, all that remains is the Curwen Arms at the foot of Ramsey Brow. The car park outside Marks & Spencer has replaced the dozen or so two-storey terraced houses on the west side of Bridge Street and most of Udale Street which lay behind them. The road itself has also been widened to accommodate the increase in traffic along Washington Street.

The Tognarelli Ice Cream factory on the east side of Bridge Street shortly before its demolition in the 1970s. Opened just after the Second World War, the premises were formerly occupied by Poole's Dairy. The Italian family who became particularly famous in the town for their classic white ice cream had settled in Workington around 1902. The business was established by brothers Ferruccio and Philip, who were assisted by their respective wives Annunziata and Germana. At one time, the family had shops in Station Road, Bridge Street, Finkle Street, Pow Street and New Oxford Street. Later the business passed to their children Harry and Renzo who thereafter traded as H & R Tognarelli.

Crowds line either side of Washington Street on a bright and sunny Sunday afternoon in 1914, to say their farewells and salute the local soldiers going off to fight in the First World War. This initial group of soldiers was later joined by around 1,500 other Workingtonians who gallantly fought in the conflict. Just over 600 were subsequently killed or later died from their wounds and never returned home. This photograph, looking north, was probably taken from the first floor balcony of the New Crown Hotel on the corner of Jane Street.

Looking north along Park End Road, *c.* 1909. This street was once simply called the Row, but was renamed sometime around 1904. It takes its name from Park End, the large detached house at its Ramsey Brow end, now the Helena Thompson Museum. Early census records tell us that the majority of residents of the Row were miners or manual workers. Yet after the large and elegant three-storey houses were built along its west side in 1881–82, it attracted some of the more wealthy and prominent townspeople.

The long flight of steps from Millfield up to Stainburn on the south side of the Yearl. There has been a watermill on this side of the River Derwent since at least the fourteenth century and the Yearl provided the head of water required to turn the waterwheels. During Victorian times it was very popular with townspeople for Sunday afternoon walks along the river through Hall Park and Millfield to escape from the dust and grim of industrial Workington. Many of the earlier pupils of Workington Grammar School (opened in 1954) will perhaps recall that the cross-country course through the park always included a gruelling climb up these seemingly endless steps.

A view of the lower section of Wilson Street looking north along Bridge Street, *c.* 1912 (see also p. 38). This clearly illustrates the major improvements that have been carried out to widen the roads in this part of the town. On the right-hand side of the street we can just see the bottom of Ramsey Brow and the corner of the Curwen Arms. This junction was obviously quite a narrow thoroughfare until the large block of property projecting out into Wilson Street (in the centre of the picture) was removed.

A photograph of the Old Market Place viewed from the lower end of King Street and looking north towards the top of Wilson Street, *c.* 1912. Sometimes also called High Market Place, weekly butter markets were once held here until around 1890. After this date, control of all markets in the town passed from the Lord of the Manor to the Borough Council. The large building on the left projecting into Market Place and obscuring our view of the top of Upper Jane Street was the Carlisle City and District Bank. In 1896 this local bank, with its headquarters in Carlisle, was taken over by the London and Midland Bank. Following negotiations with the Corporation, the bank was demolished in 1916 and replaced with a new building set back in line with the other properties on the south side of Market Place. By 1923, the London and Midland Bank had become more commonly known as simply the Midland Bank and eventually also acquired the Cumberland Union Bank in Pow Street. Their Market Place branch was closed and all its business transferred to Pow Street. More recently the Midland Bank has merged with HSBC and changed its name once more.

*Above:* Looking south up Wilson Street, towards the Old Market Place, *c.* 1912. A large detached block of property then existed at the top of the street on its west side. Edward Stevens had his grocers shop here around 1892, but by 1901 the business had been acquired by the Cooper family. For many years the building also accommodated Thomas Grisenthwaite's drapery. Against the gable end of the old grocers shop can be seen the granite water fountain presented to the town by shipbuilder Charles Lamport.

*Above:* Looking north along Washington Street, towards its junction with Jane Street. Everything here has now totally disappeared. Today the Washington Central Hotel occupies the site of the New Crown Hotel on the right of the picture and the Old Crown Hotel, opposite, was purchased by the Borough Council in 1937 in order to widen the junction. To the left of the photograph is the former County Drapery Store, built by John L. Yeowart during the early 1800s. It later became a motor garage ran by the Gordon family. One of the petrol pumps can be seen in a recess almost on the kerbside.

*Right:* Herbert Smith's chemist shop on the north side of Upper Jane Street. Herbert (1870-1935) was the eldest son of Edward and Betsy Ann Smith who lived at No. 68 Guard Street. During the 1880s the couple ran a private school at the Good Templars Hall in Station Road. One of their first pupils was their son, who later trained as a pharmacist.

*Opposite:* The wine and spirit department of the Workington Brewery Co. on the corner of Upper Jane Street, facing onto the old Market Place. In addition to the large brewery buildings on Ladies Walk (see pp 76-77), the company also handled one of the most comprehensive stocks of wine and spirits in the North of England. This Market Place property occupied much of the north side of Upper Jane Street and included several large warehouses, which extended through to the top end of Wilson Street.

Looking north along Washington Street, from a position almost opposite St John's church, *c.* 1912. The Old Crown Inn and New Crown Hotel can be seen on the left side of the street, either side of the junction with Jane Street (see previous page).

Washington Street, Workington

Jane Street looking west down towards Central Square, *c.* 1935. The *Oxford Picture House* can be seen in the distance, while the large block of property on the left-hand side of the street was the main branch and headquarters of the Workington and District Industrial and Provident Co-operative Society. Originally established as a simple grocery shop in 1865, the co-operative society grew rapidly and their Jane Street branch contained drapery, milliners, tailors and outfitters, furnishing and boot and shoe departments. Above which they also had a large café and several function rooms which catered for weddings and dances.

The front elevation of the former Conservative Club on the north side of Oxford Street, close to Central Square. Built in 1902, this attractive three-storey building with its red ashlar sandstone façade is to be demolished to make way for the latest town centre redevelopment. The town's Conservative Club has moved to new premises within the former Sunday school rooms at the rear of the United Reform church in South William Street.

*Above:* Looking west along Oxford Street during the mid-1950s. To the left is the *Oxford Picture House* on the corner of Gray Street. Opened in September 1923, the cinema was built by Issac Dockray Graves. Within its arcade-like entrance were a café and a dress shop. In 1929, the first 'talking picture' screened in West Cumberland was shown at the Oxford. Around 1,500 people visited the cinema to see *Singing Fool* starring Al Jolson.

*Right:* The old *Oxford Cinema* on the corner of Oxford Street and Gray Street, in the mid-1970s. Around this time, the Graves family remodelled the building to accommodate the Rendezvous nightclub in the main auditorium, with the Trader Bills disco above and a German-style Beer Keller in the basement. The attractive 1920s façade of the old cinema was then almost entirely clad with industrial-style steel sheeting. This large expanse of bronze coloured vertical cladding was eventually removed quarter of a century later, when the premises were converted into the Henry Bessemer public house, by J.D Wetherspoon.

A sketch of the Ritz Cinema which once stood on the north corner of Murray Road and Upton Street. This massive new 1,350-seater cinema, completed in 1938, was designed by local architect Thomas Nicholson for Graves Cinemas Ltd. Externally the building was predominately red rustic brickwork complemented with large areas of cream earthenware tiling. There were two large neon 'RITZ' signs, either side of the curved canopied front entrance. The cinema was particularly famous for its rich and elaborate Art Deco styled interior, designed by John Alexander & Sons (of Newcastle).

*Opposite above:* The former workhouse (or poorhouse) building at Ellerbeck, viewed from the north, *c.*1890. The workhouse closed in the mid-1840s, when Workington became part of the Cockermouth Union. Thereafter, the towns 'poor, less fortunate and orphaned' were accommodated at Cockermouth's new Gallowbarrow workhouse. Ellerbeck was purchased by the Borough Council in 1888 and converted into an isolation hospital. Throughout Victorian Britain frequent epidemics of cholera, smallpox, typhoid, scarlet fever and diphtheria were prevalent. There ware no vaccinations, nor antibiotics to treat these highly infectious and potentially fatal diseases. Isolation away from the community was the only way to control and prevent major epidemics. Once mass immunisation programmes were introduced the need for such hospitals declined. The main buildings at Ellerbeck were afterwards converted into a geriatric unit and a convalescent ward. Today little remains of the hospital, apart from the neat red-brick administration block which is now a private house. The site is now the small secluded private housing estate known as Ellerbeck Close.

*Right:* The bandstand in Vulcans Park, shortly before its demolition in the 1980s. This eight-sided oak structure with a green Borrowdale slate roof was officially opened on 27 July 1929. Designed by the Borough Surveyor, it was built by local contractor Joseph W. Douglas (of John Street). During the summer months brass bands regularly performed on Sunday afternoons within the park and attracted large audiences. Many were assembled from the employees at the bands local collieries and ironworks, while military bands would also occasionally entertain the crowds.

Looking east along Harrington Road from almost outside the cemetery, *c.* 1948. The large property on the left is Mossdale House which was once the home and surgery of Dr Eadie and then later became the offices of the Borough of Workington Education Commitee. In the distance is the substantial sandstone railway bridge which once crossed the road a few yards west of its junction with John Street and Mason Street.

The east side of the arched stone railway bridge which carried the tracks of the old Cleator and Workington Junction Railway over Harrington Road, photographed shortly before its demolition in 1981. The bridge was removed as it had become a major hazard to traffic, being only 4.2m (14ft) at its centre and reducing dramatically to around 3m (10ft) on each side. Tall vehicles such as double-decker buses could only safely pass under the bridge by using the centre of the road, thereby restricting the carriageway. One veteran bus driver told how they were warned to 'line the radiator cap of the bus up with the white line down the centre of the road' in order to avoid hitting the bridge.

The large warehouse of wholesale grocers J. Lindsay & Sons, on the east side of John Street, *c.* 1949. This extensive business was started by John Lindsay in April 1881, when he opened a small grocery shop in Stanley Street. Two years later he moved to a newly-built shop in Gladstone Street. The John Street warehouse opened in 1908, but originally only occupied No. 129. Twelve years later the family business acquired the former Liberty Printing Works next door, thereby doubling their floor space.

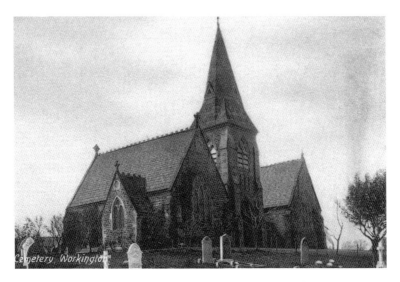

The two mortuary chapels (demolished in the 1970s) which once stood in the centre of Harrington Road cemetery. Erected in 1878, the chapels were located on either side of a covered archway, below the central bell tower and four-sided spire. One was set aside for Anglican funerals, with the other serving non-conformist burials. The arrangement was quite similar to the two chapels which still exist today at Cockermouth.

Crowds gather on the site of Workington's new infirmary, to witness the laying of the foundation stone by Edward Darcy Curwen in August 1885. The building designed by local architect George D. Oliver, initially had three wards and accommodated twelve male and four female beds. Local doctors gave their services voluntarily and Dr Charles McKerrow was appointed the first medical officer at the hospital. The nursing staff then consisted of a matron assisted only by a day and night nurse. The first patient was Robert Armstrong who was admitted on 31 December 1886. He was employed at the New Yard Ironworks and had been buried under a badly stacked quantity of pig iron. When freed he was rushed to the infirmary but died a few hours later having never regained consciousness. Harrington Road cemetery can be seen immediately behind the crowds, quite devoid of gravestones as it had only opened in 1879. It is interesting to note the open undeveloped fields on the other side of Harrington Road where Victoria Road and its surrounding streets were later built.

The original buildings of the old Workington Infirmary, viewed from the west, *c.* 1905. Its location at the end of Infirmary Road is identified on the plan at the beginning of this book (see p. 2) by the letter W. The hospital was formally opened on 29 November 1886 by Mrs A. Wilson. She was the widow of George Wilson, the former managing director of Charles Cammell and Co. and the principle driving force behind the establishment of the town's first infirmary. Sadly he died in December 1885 and never see the project completed. In its early days, the hospital was supported entirely by voluntary contributions, the workers of the district paying 'one old penny a week' to maintain the infirmary.

An aerial photograph of Bankfield viewed from the south west in 1978. This enormous property was essentially two large semi-detached houses, with separate entrances at each end. The floor plans were very similar, but at the north end was a tall tower. Across the entire top floor of the mansion was a large single room used as a ballroom or function room for special occasions. It was reached from one of two ornate staircases within each residence.

*Opposite below:* During the First World War much of Bankfield was used as a military hospital to care for wounded local soldiers returning from the front. The mansion was only then partially occupied by the Iredale and Smith families, and was made available following the death of Reginald Iredale Smith. He was the grandson of brewery owner, Peter Iredale (1828-1906), and was killed in action on the Somme in August 1916. Three recuperating soldiers pose for this interesting photograph of the interior of the makeshift hospital. Amidst the parlour palms, a nurse sits at a highly-polished table.

*Above:* The elegant mansion of Bankfield once stood in its own extensive grounds, high above Banklands and close to the east end of Newlands Lane. The site is identified on the location plan at the beginning of this book (see p. 2) by the letter R. Completed in October 1876 it was built for the prominent ironmasters Peter Kirk and Charles James Valentine, by local contractor Richard Schofield. Later it was acquired by Peter Iredale, the managing director of the Workington Brewery Co. Ltd. The Iredale family subsequently sold Bankfield to the Borough Council in 1944 and it was let as office accommodation to the National Coal Board. After being allowed to fall into major disrepair, it was finally demolished in August 1980.

Men and children collect coal during the 1912 coal strike from an outcrop below St Michael's Road. The terraced houses on the west side of Ashton Street can be seen in the distance. This photograph by William Carruthers Lawrie is one of several which graphically capture the struggle of the townspeople to find fuel for heating and cooking, at a time before homes had any electricity supply. It also illustrates just how close some coal measures are to the surface. Without doubt this exposed coal would have been exploited by earlier inhabitants of the town, many centuries before.

Another photograph taken by William Carruthers Lawrie during the coal strike of March 1912. Local families in desperate need of fuel were allowed to collect some coke from the Corporation's gas works in Stanley Street. This was strictly rationed and a policeman can be seen in the centre of the picture overseeing the distribution.

# three

# Industries

An aerial photograph of the remains of Jane Pit on Moss Bay Road, viewed from the south in 1999. The site of Jane Pit is identified on the location plan at the beginning of this book (see p. 2) by the letter T. These two tall stone chimneys and the castellated oval engine house are all that remain of Workington's once rich coal industry. Up until the latter part of the eighteenth century it was of primary commercial importance. Without its coal reserves it is unlikely that the town and port of Workington would have seen any major development. Jane Pit was sunk by the Curwen family in 1843, with production starting three years later. By 1851, the annual output was in excess of 10,000 tons with its workings extending 135m (442ft) below the surface. Much of this coal was then exported from Workington harbour, the majority of it to Ireland. In 1864 the pit was leased to William Irving who later sank the nearby Annie Pit. Jane Pit is believed to have closed around 1875.

Perhaps the only surviving photograph of the head gear of Jane Pit. This coal pit connected underground with the nearby Annie Pit and in its later days little or no coal was raised at Jane. However, its engine house was retained and used to pump water from the workings. The large flywheel of the steam engine can be seen to the left of the picture. A colourful 1883 account of the abandoned pit tells us that 'the machinery is rhematic, and the engine house, castellated chimneys and all, look as frowzy as a drunken man who has slept in a haystack'.

The pithead winding gear of the Solway Colliery viewed from the north east, with the Derwent blast furnaces in the distance, *c*. 1972. Solway Colliery was located to the south west of the Ellis Sports ground, off Moss Bay Road. Its site is identified on the location plan at the beginning of this book (see p. 2) by the letter U. It was sunk in 1937 by the United Steel Companies who operated the iron and steelworks on the opposite side of the main Whitehaven to Workington railway line. An overhead conveyor was constructed over the railway in order that the coal raised from the pit could be easily conveyed to the coke ovens at the ironworks.

*Opposite above:* The pithead of No. 3 shaft of St Helen's colliery at Siddick, *c*. 1925. Coal was then raised from a depth of around 412m, with much of the workings extending well out under the sea into the Solway Firth. At this time, the pit employed upwards of 1,500 people and was said to supply 'nine-tenths of the inhabitants of the town' with coal for heating and cooking. In 1947, when pits were nationalised, St Helen's was acquired by the National Coal Board. Production at Siddick ceased in July 1966.

*Opposite below:* St Helen's colliery at Siddick, viewed from the south in 1956. The main railway line out of Workington is seen running north to Maryport. The massive spoil heap to the left of the picture was once a very familiar landmark to those travelling between the two towns. It rose to over 55m (180ft) high and was estimated to contain 1.4 million cubic feet of burnt and unburnt shale, the waste from the mine workings. During the early 1970s, major reclamation work was carried out by the Borough Council on the former industrial sites at Oldside. The entire area, which included the colliery, its spoil heap and the old ironworks sites nearer the harbour, were landscaped.

The relatively modern underground workings of the Solway Colliery. Costing in the region of £486,000 the pit was an integral part of the iron and steel works, supplying much of the coal used in the coke ovens. After the coal industry was nationalised in 1947, the colliery passed to the National Coal Board. When it closed in 1973 it signalled the end of coal mining in the town.

*Opposite below:* A sketch looking east towards the outer area of the Low Shipyard, on the south bank of the River Derwent estuary, west of the Dock Quay. Its site is identified on the location plan at the beginning of this book (see p. 2) by the letter F. From this shipyard, Richard Williamson & Son built and launched around twenty-three new sailing ships, seventy-five steamships and over fifty steel barges or smaller vessels, between 1881 and 1938. The small circular stone tidewatchers building, with its domed roof, to the right of the picture can still be seen today. Often this lookout post is mistakenly identified as Billy Bumley House (see p. 84). The oval ball on the tall post in the centre was raised and lowered to indicate the depth of water in the river channel leading to the harbour entrance.

From around 1760, shipbuilding was a prominent industry in the town, next only in importance to the coal trade. Workington's shipyards built around 330 new sailing ships during the next century, providing regular and valuable employment for generations of workers. This was the era of the graceful timber sailing ship and the town's skilled shipbuilders were much in demand. This painting by the talented artist Joseph Heard shows the three-masted Schooner *Owen Potter* built in 1850 at Workington. Heard, who was born in Egremont in 1810, trained with a flourishing school of maritime painters based in Whitehaven, before eventually moving to Liverpool. Here he made a good living painting maritime scenes and ship portraits, receiving many commissions from his native West Cumberland.

From the mid-nineteenth century, more and more new ships were built of iron and steel rather than timber, and steam power replaced sail. Traditional shipbuilding gradually declined in the town and many skilled workers migrated to other parts of the country to seek work. In 1881 Richard Williamson & Son took over the Low Shipyard and soon diversified their operation to construct iron vessels. Their first ships were still fully rigged and sail powered and very much resembled the larger timber sailing ships of the past. This picture shows the *Scale Force*, built by Williamson in 1883. This 229 ton ship was supplied to W.S. Kennaugh and Co., who were based at Whitehaven. She was one of nine vessels built for this company at Workington and named after Lake District waterfalls.

The *Thomas Dear* built at Workington by R. Williamson &Son in 1918. Originally ordered by the Admiralty, the 200 ton vessel was later renamed the *Ninette*, and is seen leaving Gloucester harbour.

A 1929 aerial photograph of the inner area of the Low shipyard at Workington, then operated by Richard Williamson & Son Ltd. New vessels were generally launched stern first into the Dock Quay. The quayside can be seen in the top right of the picture (see p. 85), the edge of the Prince of Wales Dock can be seen in the top left. The ship under construction was the 1,131 ton *Silvonia*, launched in February 1930. It was built for the Northwest Shipping Co. which was owned by the Williamson family themselves.

A photograph of the last ever ship to be built at Workington by Richard Williamson & Son Ltd. The company started work on the 829 ton vessel in 1932, but it was never fully completed. The partially finished ship stood for many years in Williamson shipyard, close to the Dock Quay on the south side of the harbour channel. It was eventually purchased by the Goole Shipbuilding and Engineering Co. and finally launched on 2 April 1938. It was completed for F.T. Everard Co. (of London) and named the *Sodality*.

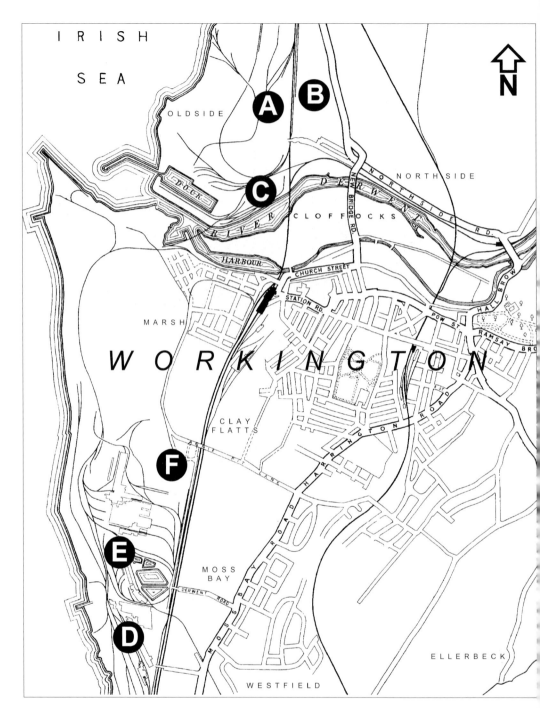

In addition to the Seaton Ironworks at Barepot, there were six other specific sites within the town where iron or steel were manufactured. The location of each works is identified on this map. (A) Workington Haematite Iron Co. (B) West Cumberland Haematite Iron Co. (C) North of England Haematite Iron Co. or Lowther Works. (D) Moss Bay Haematite Iron Co. (E) Derwent Haematite Iron Co., later Charles Cammell & Co. (F) New Yard Iron Works.

Seaton Works near Workington

Pub.d by J. Mordy, Workington.

John Mordy's early engraving of Seaton Ironworks at Barepot, viewed from Millfield on the other side of the River Derwent, *c.* 1850. This was the site of the town's first commercial ironworks and foundry, opened in the 1760s. A long row of terraced workers cottages can be seen in the foreground, Derwent House is to the right. A succession of works managers are known to have lived in this large detached property. On the hillside in the distance are the coke ovens. (Joyce Byers Collection)

The former Workington Haematite Iron and Steel Co. Works at Oldside viewed from the south west, c. 1910. The site of this ironworks is clearly identified on the plan on p. 68, by the letter A. Opened in 1856, the company started life as the Workington Haematite Iron Co. and originally operated six blast furnaces. Only three of these then remained and were used principally to smelt spiegel or ferro-manganese alloys, used in steelmaking. In 1909 the plant had been transferred to the Workington Iron and Steel Co., soon afterwards these works were renamed the Oldside Iron and Steel Works.

The six blast furnaces of the West Cumberland Iron and Steel Co. Works at Oldside viewed from the north west corner of the site, c. 1889. The location of this ironworks is clearly identified on the plan on p. 68, by the letter B, and was situated directly opposite the Workington Haematite Ironworks on the other side of the Workington-Maryport railway line. Opened in 1862, this company expanded rapidly and survived until the recession of 1892.

The blast furnaces of the Moss Bay Ironworks viewed from the south east, *c.* 1895. The site of this ironworks is identified on the plan on p. 68, by the letter D. The blast furnaces and chimneys of the Derwent Works can be seen in the distance. Moss Bay was established in 1872 by Peter Kirk and Charles James Valentine who operated the smaller Quayside Forge in Stanley Street. Steelmaking began here in June 1877, and the first steel rail order was produced two months later. Railway lines are still rolled at Moss Bay today, using basically the same techniques, albeit with the benefit of modern technology.

A white hot ingot or bloom of steel is passed back and forth through a series of specially designed heavy rollers in the rolling mill at Moss Bay. This was likened to a huge mangle, similar to that once used by every household on washing day. The process basically squeezes and shapes the ingot into a long rail. (Michael Burridge Collection)

The interior of the Bessemer steel plant at Charles Cammell and Co.'s Derwent Works, *c.* 1890. A Bessemer converter vessel can be seen to the left of the photograph. Here pig iron was converted to steel by blowing a blast of air through the molten metal. The converter was then tipped forward and the newly-made steel was transferred into a large ladle. This revolved over the circular casting pit seen to the bottom left of the picture. It was then carefully poured (or teemed) into the rows of empty ingot moulds standing upright in the pit. (Michael Burridge Collection)

The blast furnaces of the Derwent Ironworks in the 1950s, viewed from the east with the reservoirs in the foreground. The site of this ironworks is identified on the plan on p. 68, by the letter E. Pig iron production began here in June 1875 and continued to be smelted on this site for another century. The three blast furnaces are located in the centre of the photograph, either side of which are the rows of tall regenerative stoves used to pre-heat the air blast. Each blast furnace was a different size, ranging from 4.8m (15.75ft) to 6m (20ft) in diameter.

Guests gather on specially-erected stands to witness the visit of King George V and Queen Mary to the Workington Iron and Steel plant in May 1917. The blast furnaces of the Moss Bay Works can be seen in the background. During these war years, George V was seen as very much a 'people's King' making frequent trips to the battlefields of France. At home, his morale-boosting visits to important munition plants such as Moss Bay were to encourage 'hearts and hands of the workers playing a different, but yet equally vital part' in the bitter conflict.

King George V dressed in his khaki military uniform was escorted around the plant by the works manager, Thomas W. Graham (left) and Joseph Valentine Ellis (centre). Queen Mary was accompanied by the town's MP, Sir John Randles. During the visit the royal party were shown a blast furnace being tapped and watched the molten iron flow into the pig beds. They also witnessed a Bessemer blow, the King commenting that this magnificent spectacle was 'one of the best things he had seen that day'.

A 1950s photograph of High Brewery, looking west from below Hall Brow. Established in 1792, the brewery changed hands several times until it was eventually acquired by John Iredale in 1839. It remained in the Iredale family, passing after his death to his sons Thomas, Peter and John. In 1891, the family converted the business into a limited company and thereafter it traded as the Workington Brewery Co. Up until its acquisition by Matthew Brown Ltd during the 1970s, the brewery was famous for its John Peel brand of beers, which included Bitter, Mild, Golden Bitter, Pale Ale and Brown Ale. It is interesting to note that each of the brewery's dray wagons was named after one of the hounds of the famous huntsman John Peel.

THE WORKINGTON BREWERY COMPANY LIMITED

JOHN PEEL

"at last"

PALE ALE

CUMBERLAND

*Above:* Interior photograph of the main bottling room at the Workington Brewery in Ladies Walk, *c.* 1955. Here the empty beer bottles were first washed and scoured clean, before being carried on a conveyor to the filling machine. Once filled with beer from a storage tank, the bottles were capped and passed through the labeller, where each paper label was gummed and stuck to the bottle. Finally, they were lifted by hand into the wooden crates. Up to ten workers were continuously employed on this bottle line.

*Left:* A sketch based on the design for the beer bottle labels of the Workington Brewery Co., *c.* 1950. The bottling plant at the High Brewery then produced four main beers: Pale Ale, Old Ale, Export and Stout. The labels featuring the famous huntsman were all of the same basic design, but printed in different colours for each type of beer. The Pale Ale label had a white background, the illustration was yellow and red with black lettering.

The Brothwell & Mills' Imperial Cordial and Mineral Water factory in Fletcher Street, *c.* 1911. This business was established in 1884 by George Henry Brothwell and James Mills. Both were staunch supporters of the temperance movement and their primary aim was to curb the consumption of alcohol, particularly among the working classes. The business survived for over a century, and many older readers will no doubt still remember their bottles of lemonade and cream soda for sale in almost every corner shop throughout the town.

four

# Transport

Thomas Benson's photograph of the South Quay at Workington harbour, *c*. 1892. Very little has changed since William Barlett's engraving, reproduced on pages 18 and 19, recorded a similar scene in 1837. However, the coal hurries had disappeared from the quayside as Workington then had no operational coal pits to the south of the River Derwent. Any coal still produced at St Helen's was shipped from Lonsdale Dock. The paddle steamer in the foreground is indicative of the transition from sailing ships to steam-powered vessels.

The older part of Workington harbour looking almost due west and perhaps taken from the tower of St Michael's church, *c.* 1919. Merchants Quay can be seen to the far right, with the South Quay in the centre of the picture on the opposite side of the South Gut.

ESTUARY

SITE OF SHIPBUILDING YARDS

DOCK QUAY

---- SOUTH QUAY

SOUTH GUT

An aerial photograph of the port of Workington, viewed from the south east in 1999. The River Derwent flows from the right, past the entrance to the old harbour. Here the South Quay and the Merchants Quay were located on either side of the South Gut. The river or beck flowing into the South Gut originates at the Yearl in Millfield and winds its way across Hall Park and the Cloffolks

PRINCE OF WALES DOCK

CHANTS QUAY

RIVER DERWENT

before emerging into the harbour. The Dock Quay to the left of the photograph, on the south bank of the estuary, was completed in August 1798. Originally much of the Dock Quay basin was enclosed along its south and west sides by a high quayside, similar to those along the South Quay. These walls were removed in 1967 to provide better access for pleasure craft.

A view east along the South Gut at high tide, around the turn of the century. The harbour wall of the Dock Quay can be seen to the right of the photograph. Alongside the South Quay is a dredger, employed to remove the sand and gravel from the harbour channel in order to keep the port open. Entering the South Gut in the centre is the Workington tug boat hauling a twin-masted schooner.

The famous folly, affectionately known as 'Billy Bumley House' on the south bank of the River Derwent estuary, pictured from the south. The blast furnaces and chimneys of the Oldside ironworks can be seen in the distance. The white-painted circular structure once served as a navigation point for mariners using the port. They could take bearings to other prominent landmarks, such as St Bees Head, the Peak of Ally and Borough Head in order to plot their course to and from the harbour. It is suggested that the old landmark demolished in 1960, received its name by virtue of its likeness to a beehive, although the old Cumberland dialect word for a bailiff or sheriffs officer is 'Bumbaily'. Perhaps in the past it was once also used by the locals to describe the customs officer that patrolled the coastline seeking out smugglers.

The remains of the Dock Quay at the western end of the South Quay at Workington harbour, completed in August 1798. Mainly funded by John Christian Curwen, the new larger dock allowed huge amounts of coal from his collieries to be loaded into ships and exported across the Irish Sea to Ireland. With its completion there were now over eighty mooring points along the South Quay and around the new dock. Some historic references are made to the Dock Quay as the Glebe Quay, perhaps because it was built on the former church or glebe lands, and replaced a much smaller wharf of the same name.

On 30 June 1927, the Prince of Wales (later King Edward VIII) formally open the town's new deep-water dock, after whom it was named. It was built on the site of the much smaller Lonsdale Dock which had been constructed in 1861. Here the Prince is seen crossing the new swing bridge over the South Gut, he is accompanied by the Mayor, Councillor Baines. The dock-side cranes can be seen in the distance.

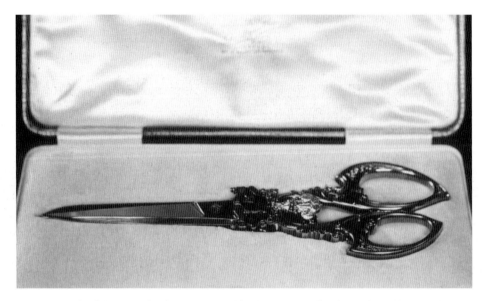

A photograph of the pair of gold scissors used by the Prince of Wales to formally open the new dock at Workington, on 30 June 1927.

*Opposite above:* A 1944 photograph of the concrete pier and breakwater on the south side of the River Derwent estuary. The Solway coastline has a very notable northwards drift and for centuries the harbour entrance has been prone to silting up with gravel and shale. In 1824, John Christian Curwen had attempted to remedy the problem by building John Pier a little further to the south, but over the years this proved ineffective. Matters were further exacerbated when the ironworks at Moss Bay began dumping slag on the foreshore. This new large concrete breakwater was built to replace John Pier and although it relieved the immediate problem, it had to be subsequently extended.

*Opposite below:* When the breakwater was extended, the pier structure was protected on either side by hundreds of large blocks of concrete. Each weighed a massive 30 tons, and measured 2.7m x 2.7m x 2.1m (8ft 9in x 8ft 9in x 7ft 0in). These were all cast by John Mowlem and Co. at a temporary plant erected on the foreshore. This photograph shows a newly-cast block being lifted by the overhead crane onto a flat railway truck. The locomotive then shunted the block along the breakwater, where it was simply dropped into place over the edge of the pier.

The Prince of Wales Dock at Workington, viewed from the east, close to the dock gates. Opened in 1927, the new dock measured 297m (975ft) long, 107m (350ft) wide at its widest point and 10.2m (33.5ft) deep at high spring tides. Unlike the earlier Lonsdale Dock which had its entrance on the north bank of the river estuary, the Prince of Wales Dock gates face west and are 21.4m (70ft) wide.

Iron ore is unloaded from the *Moldavia* at the Prince of Wales Dock. The Workington Harbour and Dock Board operated the dock until the end of 1957, thereafter it was transferred to the United Steel Companies. They created a subsidiary company known as the Workington Harbour and Dock Co. to manage the facility. A direct rail link with the iron and steel plants south of the River Derwent had existed since 1927, with the construction of the swing bridge over the entrance to the South Gut.

Workington's Central Station and approaches were elaborately decorated for Queen Alexandra's Floral Day in 1912. Alexandra, who was originally from Denmark, was the wife of King Edward VI. The event was instigated to mark the 50th anniversary of her arrival in England and raised much needed funds for hospitals throughout the country. At this time there was no National Health Service to fund the running of our hospitals.

The platform at Workington's Central Station, viewed from the south in June 1939. The Oxford Street road bridge crosses over the tracks, immediately behind the old water tower in the centre of the picture. This photograph was taken during filming of *The Stars Look Down*, a major feature film starring Michael Redgrave and Margaret Lockwood. Adapted from a novel by A.J. Cronin, the film tells the moving and tragic story of a group of coal miners buried alive through the greed of the pit owner. Other scenes were shot at Borough Park, St Helen's colliery and within the terraced streets of Northside and Clifton.

CLOFFOLKS

CARNEGIE

RITZ
CINEMA

BUS
STATION

OXFORD
CINEMA

CENTRAL
STATION

GRAY
STREET

Aerial photograph of the Central Railway Station and Oxford Street, viewed from the south in 1954. The bus station is on the left and Oxford Street runs from left to right across the centre of the picture towards Central Square. Here was Central Station, operated until 1923 by the Cleator and Workington Junction Railway. Thereafter, until its closure, the line became part of London Midland Scottish. The tracks can be clearly seen passing under the Oxford Street bridge, running north towards Siddick and Seaton.

The front elevation of the Central Station, based on the original architects drawings. This substantial two-storey building which served as the headquarters of the Cleator and Workington Junction Railway was situated just off Central Square, on the opposite side of Oxford Street to the old Conservative Club. The site of Central Station is identified on the location plan at the beginning of this book (see p. 2) by the letter P. Opened in 1878, this railway station was one of three that existed in the town until the 1930s. The others were Workington Bridge station at the foot of Clava Brow and Low Station at the bottom of Station Road.

A view along the Cleator and Workington Junction Railway line south out of Central Station, *c.* 1935. To the far right are the backs of the terraced houses on the east side of Gray Street, while in the centre of the photograph is the signal box and large engine shed belonging to the railway company. Today, much of this site accommodates the Central Square car park. Opened in 1878, the C&WJR ran south through Harrington, Distington and Moresby Parks, to join the Furnace Railway at Cleator Moor. North out of Workington the line ran through Seaton, to join the Maryport and Carlisle Railway at Linefoot. Although passenger trains also worked the line, it was built predominately to supply iron ore and coal to the various ironworks within the town.

# CLEATOR AND WORKINGTON JUNCTION RAILWAY.

| UP TRAINS. | | am | am | pm | pm | pm | |
|---|---|---|---|---|---|---|---|
| Moor Row | .... | 7 45 | 10 0 | 2 15 | .. | 6 20 | THE |
| Cleator Moor | .... | 7 49 | 10 4 | 2 19 | .. | 6 24 | |
| Moresby Parks | .... | 7 57 | 1012 | 2 26 | .. | 6 32 | Embassy Note, |
| Distington | .... | 8 5 | 1020 | 2 34 | .. | 6 40 | |
| High Harrington | ..de | 8 9 | 1024 | 2 38 | .. | 6 44 | 1/- for 5 quires. |
| Workington—Central Station | 8 15 | 1029 | 2 43 | .. | 6 49 | | |
| Siddick Junction | .. | 8 17 | 1035 | 2 49 | .. | 6 55 | W. PAGEN, Whitehaven. |

| DOWN TRAINS. | | am | pm | pm | pm | p.m. | |
|---|---|---|---|---|---|---|---|
| Siddick Junction | .. | 8 25 | 1211 | 5 0 | | 7 0 | |
| Workington —Central Station | 8 35 | 1217 | 5 5 | 7B 5 | 8A35 | | HENRY & MARY, |
| High Harrington | .. | 8 40 | 1222 | 5 10 | 7 10 | 8 40 | |
| Distington | .. | ..de | 8 44 | 1226 | 5 14 | 7 14 | 8 44 |
| Moresby Parks | .. | 8 52 | 1234 | 5 22 | 7 22 | 8 52 | 1/-. |
| Cleator Moor .. | .. | 9 0 | 1242 | 5 30 | 7 30 | 9 0 | |
| Moor Row | .. | 9 5 | 1247 | 5 35 | 7 34 | 9 5 | W. PAGEN, Whitehaven. |

A daily timetable for passenger trains calling at Workington's Central Station, reproduced from the 1893 *West Cumberland Railway Guide* published by William Pagen of Whitehaven. Rail travellers going further afield could join the London North Western Railway at Siddick Junction or the Furness Railway at Moor Row. As the Cleator and Workington Junction Railway had been established essentially as a mineral line to transport iron ore and coal, it had no locomotives or carriages to operate passenger trains. So from their earliest beginnings they entered into an agreement with the larger Furness Railway Co. who provided the necessary rolling stock and worked all the passenger traffic on their behalf. The last passenger train between Workington and Cleator Moor ran in April 1931.

Railway staff (and others) pose for the photographer outside the Cleator and Workington Junction Railway goods shed, *c.* 1910. This large predominantly timber building was located adjacent to Central Station, its gable end facing north onto the station approaches. In later years, the building was used as a vehicle repair workshop before its demolition during the 1990s.

*Brigham Hill,* a 0-6-0 saddle tank locomotive operated by the Cleator & Workington Junction Railway. This steam engine was employed in and around the town, hauling coal and iron ore between the pits, the ironworks and the Lonsdale Dock. This particular locomotive derived its name from the residence of William Fletcher, who was a director of the railway company and lived at Brigham Hill, near Cockermouth. Several C&WJR engines were named after the homes of company directors.

Workington Iron & Steel Co. locomotive no. 69. A 0-4-0 saddle tank steam engine built at the Robert Stephenson Locomotive works. This engine operated in and around the works, and to and from the Prince of Wales Dock, transporting coal and iron ore. (Helena Thompson Museum)

Workington Bridge which crosses the River Derwent at the foot of Calva Brow, viewed from the south west, c. 1895. Built in 1841 by Thomas Nelson (of Carlisle), this substantial yellow sandstone bridge replaced an earlier structure which was located a little further upstream, opposite Workington Hall Mill. To the right of the picture is the Bridge Station signal box, the main station buildings were across the road, on the other side of the bridge approaches. A 0-6-0 steam locomotive stands in the foreground.

Workington Bridge Station viewed from the west, c. 1930. This railway station was located at the foot of Calva Brow on the parapet of the road bridge over the River Derwent. The site of this station is identified on the location plan at the beginning of this book (see p. 2) by the letter N. The main station buildings are in the centre of the photograph on the south side of the line. Externally, the lower part of the station at platform level was built of stone, with upper floor boarded in timber. Passengers entered this upper level, which housed the ticket office and stationmasters office, from the road before descending a long flight of steps onto the platform. Opened in September 1881, this station replaced an earlier structure on the opposite side of the tracks.

Looking north along Murray Road, mid-1950s. On the left is the red-brick façade of the bus station, built in 1926 and said to be the first purpose-built covered bus station in England. The large department store next door was Brownes, opened in 1936 and operated by the Whitehaven Beehive. In the far distance, at the junction of Murray Road and Pow Street was the large three-storey Clydesdale Bank building, opened around 1880.

Looking north across a busy Central Square, 1924. Opened around 1883, the Central Hotel was built by William Coulthard. One feature of this once prominent Workington Hotel was its elaborate cast iron glazed entrance porch, which extended over the pavement. Below its glazed hipped roof was the name of the hotel picked out in attractive stained and coloured glass. The vehicle in the centre is a single deck bus, typical of those operated by Cumberland Motor Services in the 1920s.

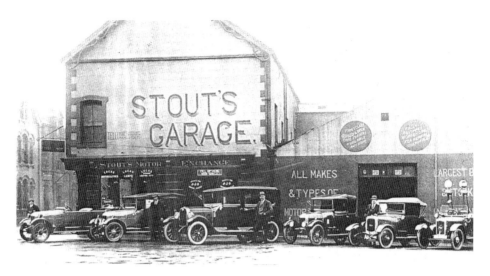

Stout's Garage on the south side of Central Square, *c.* 1923. These premises were originally built for the Derwent Engineering Co., established in 1904 by the Quirk family. Motoring was still very much in its infancy and a motor car was a rare sight on the streets of the town. John Fletcher Stout purchased the Quirk's motor engineering business just before the First World War. When he died in 1933, Stout's was described as the largest motor dealership in the north west, with branches in Whitehaven and Egremont.

A delivery van belonging to Jarman & Sons of the Belvedere Street Dairy. The Jarman family moved to the town from Dronfield, when Charles Cammell and Co. relocated their steelworks to Workington in 1883. As well as the dairy, the family also ran a number of successful greengrocers and fruit shops. In 1928 their Pow Street shop was one of those destroyed by the fire which engulfed the Opera House.

A visit to Workington by famous French aviator, Maurice Ducroq brought a great deal of public interest and excitement. This photograph by W.C. Lawrie records his take-off from Millfield during one of his flights over the town on Saturday 20 August 1911. The aeroplane is a 50hp Gnome-powered Farman biplane. On this occasion he is recorded as following Northside Road, passing over the Lowther Ironworks, before flying out to sea for about two miles. On his return be crossed over the steelworks at Moss Bay, and then flew north to make a perfect landing in the centre of Lonsdale Park.

Two years after Ducroq's visit to Workington, Gustav Hamel gave a flying display at the 1913 Workington Sports. Some 14,000 people filled Lonsdale Park to see one of Britain's foremost pilots. This photograph, again taken by W.C. Lawrie shows Hamel in the long raincoat standing in front of his 80hp Gnome-powered Blériot monoplane in the centre of Lonsdale Park. Unfortunately he only made one flight that day which almost proved fatal. After taking off from Lonsdale Park, he made a wide sweep over Oldside and upon his return noticed the spectators had swarmed over his landing area. In severe headwinds he aborted his approach and flew seawards again intending to land on the beach. But Hamel doubted he could land safely when he discovered the beach was mainly shingle and gravel, so he ditched his aircraft into the sea as close as possible to the shore. Wading safely ashore, he was assisted by hundreds of onlookers who helped pull his aeroplane out of the rough sea.

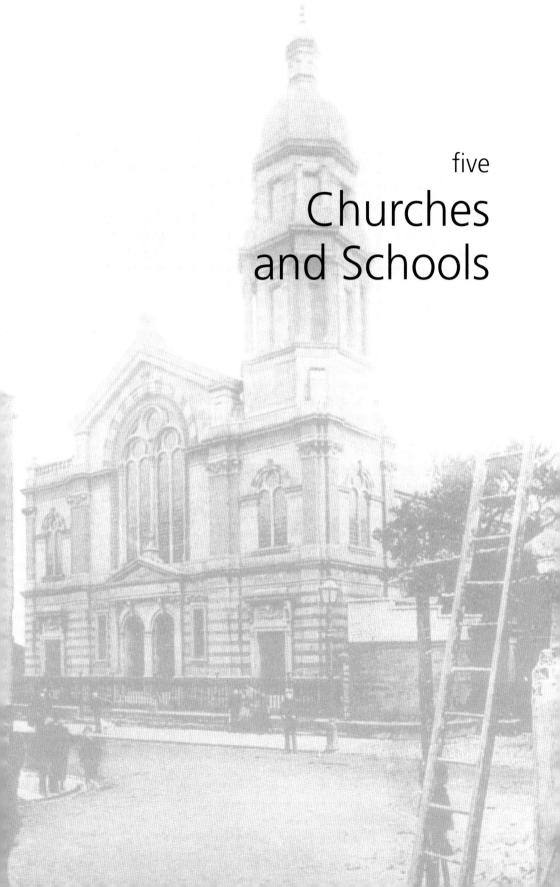

five
# Churches
# and Schools

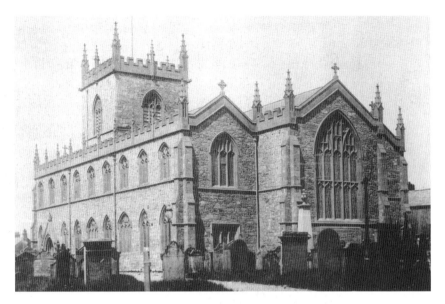

Thomas Benson's photograph of St Michael's parish church at Workington, viewed from the east, *c.* 1892. A place of worship has existed on this site since at least the ninth century, but the structure of the church has changed several times. The oldest remaining part is the lower section of its square Norman tower. This Early English-style church was designed by Bassett Smith (of London) and James Howes (of Workington) and replaced the Georgian-style church destroyed by fire in 1887. Pointed gothic tracery windows replaced the rather plain round headed windows and decorative pinnacles, parapet walls and buttresses were added.

A 1923 photograph of the chancel and east window of St Michael's church. This picture records the gothic style interior of the church after it was rebuilt following the fire of 1887. Just over a century later, this church would suffer the same fate as its predecessor in the tragic fire of 1994. Virtually everything within the chancel of the church was lost forever, including the many fine stained-glass windows and the Caen stone and marble pulpit.

Within St Michael's church is an ancient stone altar tomb, with the life-size effigies of Sir Christopher Curwen and his wife Elizabeth. Sir Christopher, who died in 1453, lies upon the tomb wearing typical fifteenth-century knight's armour, beside him is his wife. The knight, who is credited with adding the Great Hall to Workington Hall, is known to have fought several times in France during the Hundred Years War. As a reward for his services, Henry VI granted him the castle and lands of Cany and Canyell in Gaux, France. When the English finally lost Normandy, the castle was recaptured by the French. In 1429 the King called Sir Christopher to arms to resist the invasions of the Scots and later as overseer of the truce with King James II of Scotland. Although the tomb today has a natural stone finish, records suggest that the stone effigies and the heraldic shields may once have been elaborately painted. Before the church was extended in 1770, the altar tomb originally stood under the square Norman tower. The above picture shows the effigy in the north east corner of the nave. It was only after the disastrous fire of 1994 that the tomb was moved to its present position. During this fire the effigy itself was seriously damaged and had to be extensively restored.

An engraving of St John's church in Washington Street, published by bookseller John Mordy around 1850. It is not quite a true depiction of the church as its tower is actually positioned centrally on the ridge of the roof. St John's was designed by Thomas Hardwick, who in 1795 had rebuilt much of St Paul's church in London's Covent Garden. The portico of this Workington church is an enlarged copy of St Paul's. Consecrated in November 1823, the building costs for St John's were met by the Church Building Society in thanksgiving for victory at the Battle of Waterloo and the end of the Napoleonic war. The square stone tower is a later addition of 1844-46.

St John's church, 1930s. A closer look at this picture reveals the high iron railings which once surrounded the church and its adjoining graveyard. During the Second World War, when there was a desperate shortage of iron for armaments and munitions manufacture the Government ordered all local authorities to requisition all unnecessary iron and steel. In 1942 the railings of St John's were removed as the Workington's streets were relentlessly stripped of their iron railings, gates and other (some now priceless) ornamental features. The majority of this ironwork found its way to the new electric-arc furnace at Chapel Bank.

*Above:* A 1927 photograph of the interior of St John's church, showing the altar located at the east end of the nave. Originally when the church was built in 1821–23, the altar was at the opposite end as it is today. This alteration was made in 1903 by Revd Robert Sanders Greene. Then the congregation entered the church via the two doors seen on either side of the altar. Canon John Croft, Greene's successor, reversed the layout of the church in 1931, and returned the altar to its present position.

*Left:* Canon John R. Croft the influential vicar of St John's church from 1914–1959. He moved to Workington from St Aidan's church in South Shields. During the First World War he served as chaplain to the Border Regiment and witnessed first hand the horrors in France and Flanders.

An interior view of St John's church looking west in the opposite direction to the previous photograph, again taken after Revd Greene's alterations. Today, this end of the church is occupied by the altar and the magnificent gilded baldachino or canopy installed under the direction of Canon Croft, and designed by Sir J. Ninian Comper.

A 1935 photograph of St John's church taken after Canon Croft's alterations and depicting much of the interior of the church we see today. The gilded baldachino in the centre forms a magnificent focal point guiding the congregation's attention to the sanctuary as they enter the church. The National Committee for the Care of Churches describes St John's as having the 'finest classical altar in England'.

Sketch of the former Wesleyan Methodist church in South William Street. Built in 1840, the church occupied the same site as today's Trinity Methodist church. The elegant Georgian building with its carefully proportioned façade, was destroyed by fire on 9 April 1889. For the second time in just over two years the town had lost another major church building. The Methodist church, not even fifty years old, had like St Michael's been totally reduced to ashes.

*Opposite:* Thomas Benson's photograph of the new Wesleyan Methodist church in South William Street, completed in 1890. It replaced the Georgian style church shown above. The architect was Charles W. Bell (of London) and the construction work cost in excess of £5,000. During the rebuilding, services were held in the old Sunday School rooms in Tiffin Lane which now form part of the Opera House building. Of particular interest is the lower part of the front elevation which was remodelled in the mid-1960s. It shows the church before the addition of the present wide glazed entrance doors and rather unsympathetic green slate panels.

A 1999 aerial photograph of Our Lady and St Michael Roman Catholic church on Banklands, viewed from the south west and built close to the first Roman Catholic chapel in the town erected in 1814. The foundation stone for this church was laid in October 1873 and it was consecrated in September 1876. It is unquestionably one the finest buildings in the town. The large pointed gothic stained-glass window, with its finely detailed mullions and tracery is dedicated to the memory of Abbot Vincent Clifton who was priest at the church for forty-six years.

*Opposite:* The façade of Our Lady and St Michael Roman Catholic church, viewed looking south from Bank Road. Constructed from Cheshire red sandstone, the belfry of this church is around 90ft high. There are several similarities between this building and the Roman Catholic churches at Whitehaven and Cleator Moor, all of which are based on the designs of Edward W. Pugin.

Thomas Benson's photograph of the Baptist church on the corner of Harrington Road and Gray Street, *c.* 1892. Formally opened in September 1886, this church was built predominantly of red ashlar sandstone, in neat horizontal courses and bands. Its façade was dominated by two tall hexagonal lead roofed 'pepper pot' towers at each corner. Between the towers was a slate roofed porch supported by three arches. Demolished in the early 1980s, the present single storey Baptist church rooms occupies the open area to the right of the picture.

*Opposite:* The former Presbyterian church in Sanderson Street opened in May 1889. It was designed in the Early English Gothic style by Charles W. Eaglesfield and replaced an earlier church on the same site first built in 1750. Then it was known as the Scotch church or High Meeting House. In 1972 the Presbyterians merged with the Congregational church and became known as the United Reform church. The Sanderson Street church last occupied by the Workington Christian Fellowship was demolished in 2003, being part of the latest town centre redevelopment.

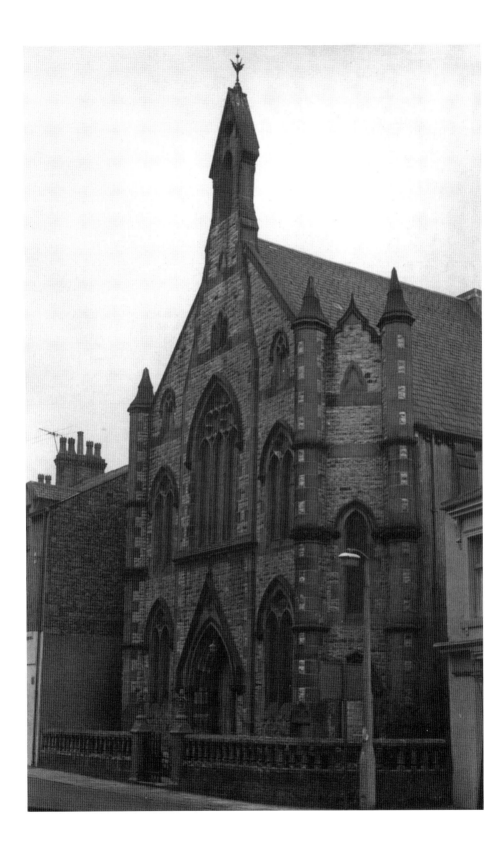

The front of St John's Church of England School, viewed from the north west across the playground in 1961. This school was located at the upper end of John Street, which then extended across Central Square to Pow Street. The two-storey building and this section of the street eventually disappeared when St John's shopping precinct was built in the late 1960s. Opened on 30 March 1860, St John's was originally built and maintained by the parish church.

St John's School, this time viewed from the bottom of Edkin Street at the opposite end of John Street, seen shortly before its closure in the late 1960s. When it closed the children were all transferred to the new Ashfield School built at the east end of Newlands Lane. In its latter years the junior school occupied much of the building including all the first floor classrooms. The infant school was located at the north end.

One of the mixed infant school classes at St John's School, *c.* 1924. Their classrooms were quite different to today's; all pupils then sat side by side on long-galleried benches facing their teacher. This arrangement was not unique to St John's, we know all eight schools managed by the Workington School Board had similar benches. It was 1926 before this system was gradually replaced with the more traditional cast iron and timber desks.

A group of St John's infant school pupils pose with their teacher in 1925. This picture was taken at the rear of the school in the north east corner of the uneven cobbled school yard. The gates to the left lead out down a short lane into Pow Street. Note the rather shabby and grubby appearance of some of the boys, suggesting they came from poor families struggling during the depression of the 1920s.

114

*Above:* The former Newlands School buildings, which were located at the east end of Newlands Lane, viewed from the south east. Completed in 1931, the school was originally called the New Central School and was a mixed secondary school. However, both male and female pupils were then taught in separate areas and sexes were strictly discouraged from mixing. By 1949 the school catered for girls only and became known as Newlands Girls Secondary School. To the right of the picture we can see the rear of Bankfield in the distance (see p. 56 and 57).

*Opposite:* Sketch of the front elevation of Guard Street School, first opened in December 1831. The central block, with its portico entrance was the original building, the remainder are later additions. Eventually the premises extended along the west side of the street, from the corner of Bank Road down to the corner of Harrington Road. The school was first established or endowed by Thomas Wilson and was often also known as Wilson School. Originally the building started life as a 'School of Industry' and an infant school. But in February 1902 a new grammar (or secondary) school was opened in the building, under the control and management of the Workington School Board.

*Following page above:* The front elevation of Workington County Technical and Secondary School in Park Lane, viewed from the west, *c.* 1930. Opened in 1912, this attractive red-brick building accommodated both the town's grammar school and the technical college, offering day, afternoon and evening classes. Over the years, the name changed several times. From 1929 it was known as the West Cumberland Secondary School and Cumberland Technical College. After 1945, it was revised to Workington Grammar School and Secondary Technical College. Nine years later, after the grammar school moved to Stainburn, it became Workington Technical College.

Technical College.
Workington.

Aerial photograph of the West Cumbria College buildings, adjacent to Vulcans Park viewed from the south east in 1999. The college closed in 2001 and transferred to new premises at Lillyhall. Workington's new hospital is presently being constructed on the site and is due to open shortly. The oldest parts of the building are to the left of the picture, facing onto Park Lane. The large eight-storey tower block in the centre dominated the Workington skyline for nearly forty years until its recent demolition.

six

# Workington
# Hall

*Above:* An interesting nineteenth-century engraving of Workington Hall, viewed from the north east. Unlike today, the steep sloping bank down to the park below is almost devoid of major trees, allowing residents of the Hall amazing views far up the River Derwent valley. The tall arched windows along this elevation were positioned in the salon and library on the first floor. The suite of bedrooms above were usually occupied by the Squire and his family.

Aerial photograph of the remains of Workington Hall, the former residence of the Curwen family, viewed from the south in 1999. Some sections of this old building date back to the fourteenth century, for example the substantial square tower at the south east corner. Unfortunately this once elegant Georgian mansion having witnessed so much of the town's history, now stands roofless and somewhat forlorn.

*Opposite below:* Thomas Benson's photograph of Workington Hall, viewed from the south, *c.* 1895. The large conservatory and vinery in the centre of the picture measured around 17.4m long by 5.2m (57ft x 17ft 2in). Records suggest it was erected sometime after 1890, although old engravings of the hall point to it replacing another similar structure. A further greenhouse extended along the remainder of the south facing wall, above this was a narrow lead-lined veranda reached via the first-floor windows of the drawing room.

*Above:* The dining room of Workington Hall, added by architect John Carr in the late eighteenth century. The primary feature of this room was its highly decorative Adam style plasterwork, particularly the cornice with its fine dentils and corbels. Carr was also responsible for detailing much of the once magnificent joinery work of the hall, including the Corinthian columns in this room. The elegant carved white marble fire surround was flanked on either side by columns of Blue John Derbyshire spar. Around the walls were fifteen very clever paintings made to resemble bias-relief plaster panels. By May 1965 virtually all this priceless work had been lost forever. One important feature of Workington Hall which is often overlooked was its superb collection of fine period furniture made by Gillow and Co. (of Lancaster). Perhaps some of the most significant pieces were the dining table with its set of fourteen Hepplewhite style chairs, together with the sideboard table and urns at the back of the room. Made in 1788, this furniture was eventually sold by the auctioneers, Christie, Manson and Wood in 1948. It has subsequently been acquired by the United States Government and it is thought to have once been used within the White House. Today, it graces the State Dining Room of the American Embassy in Vienna.

*Opposite:* Full length portrait of Isabella Curwen (1765-1820) of Workington Hall, painted by George Romney between 1782-83. Isabella, depicted on the shores of Windermere with Belle Isle in the background, was the wife of John Christian Curwen. Measuring 2.44m x 1.5m (96in x 59in) the original painting was sold by the Curwen family in 1961, and is now in a private collection in the United States. A much smaller print of this picture is displayed in the town's Helena Thompson Museum. Romney also painted a similar full-length portrait of John Christian Curwen, and both paintings once hung together in the salon at Workington Hall.

An engraving of the portrait of Mary Queen of Scots which once hung in Workington Hall. It is thought the portrait depicts the Scottish Queen at around the age of twenty-five. She is wearing a loose gown of crimson brocade, with white satin vertical decoration. Her blouse is open around the neck to show a pearl necklace and has a straight collar, embroidered and edged in gold. Upon her head is a large transparent veil falling like a mantle onto her shoulders, beneath this is a small round cap on the back of her head.

*Opposite:* An 1820 engraving from a painting by Robert Smirke, depicting Mary Queen of Scots and her party landing at Workington on Sunday 16 May 1568. After the disastrous battle of Langside, the Scottish Queen fled in a small fishing boat from Abbey Burn, on the Scottish side of the Solway. She decided to seek refuge at Workington and throw herself upon the mercy of her cousin and rival, Queen Elizabeth I. She was never to return to her beloved Scottish kingdom and spent her last night of freedom at Workington Hall. The following day, four hundred horsemen arrived at Workington and detained Mary. The artist has employed a degree of artistic licence by depicting a large stone quayside in the background of this picture. At this time Workington didn't have any recognised harbour, all goods were then simply transferred on and off vessels from the shore or river bank.

*Above:* Stadler's engraving of Schoose Farm, viewed from the south east, *c.* 1815. Schoose is located at the very top of High Street, on the east side of the road and is still a working farm today. As well as once supplying the town and Workington Hall with much of its produce, it was also an experimental farm, built by John Christian Curwen to indulge his fascination with agriculture. As the founding president of the Workington Agricultural Society, he compiled lengthy and finely detailed annual reports of his activities. Curwen was troubled that after the Enclosure Acts, British farming methods were exposed as quite naive. In addition, during this period of revolution and hostility in Europe, the country had to become much more self-sufficient at growing and feeding its population. At Schoose, he carefully assessed the benefits of different types of crops, their growing conditions and various feed for his cattle. Curwen also tested various breeds of cows and sheep, including the Spanish Merinos brought to this country by Sir Joseph Banks. He also set up an innovative feed programme for his farm and colliery horses, supplementing their winter feed with carrots and steamed potatoes.

*Above:* The restored castellated entrance to Schoose farm, viewed from the north. John Christian Curwen continued to work the farm until 1826, when he sold off all his valuable stock of short-horn cattle. The fine stone farm buildings are almost unique and remain, along with his extensive agricultural writings, a monument to this agricultural pioneer and social reformer.

A finely detailed steel engraving of John Christian Curwen (1756–1828), with Schoose Farm to his right. He was the son of John Christian (1719–1767) and Jane Curwen (the daughter of Eldred Curwen). Orphaned at just eleven years old, his uncle Henry Curwen was appointed his guardian and he spent much of his youth at Workington Hall. In October 1782, he married Henry Curwen's only surviving daughter Isabella, his first cousin, and later adopted the surname Curwen. He served as the MP for Carlisle City for over thirty years and was later elected MP for Cumberland between 1820-28.

*Above, left:* One of the most interesting architectural feature of Schoose Farm was the tall windmill, the shell of which still survives today. Built by John Christian Curwen in 1809–10, the windmill was used to provide motive power for the farm. The engraving on p. 124 suggests it once had six sails and a domed top.

*Above, right:* Another photograph of the remains of the old windmill at Schoose Farm, viewed from north. Like the majority of the other substantial farm buildings, the tower was conzstructed from pale yellow sandstone quarried close by at Castle Gardens.

*Opposite, above:* Thomas Benson's photograph of Cuckoo Arch, viewed from the south west, *c.* 1895. This semicircular arched bridge spanned the main road leading to Stainburn and linked Workington Hall to Schoose Farm. It was built around 1790, from the same locally quarried, pale yellow sandstone used to construct the Hall. Several legends surround the arch, one suggesting it to be Elizabethan, but clearly the bridge displays obvious Georgian architectural features. The once famous landmark was demolished in October 1931, as its condition had deteriorated and the narrow opening had become something of a hazard to traffic.

*Opposite, below:* The Hall lodge house at the Stainburn entrance to Hall Park, *c.* 1913. This small cottage is located a hundred yards or so east of where Cuckoo Arch stood. East Lodge on the opposite side of Stainburn Road can just be seen through the trees in the distance. Similar lodge houses are found close to the majority of entrances to the Workington Hall estates, this particular one overlooks the track leading across Hall Park to the Hall Mill.

# Other local titles published by Tempus

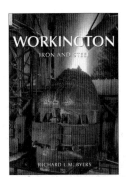

## Workington Iron and Steel
RICHARD L.M. BYERS

During the latter half of the nineteenth century, Workington became a major centre for the production of iron and steel. It was an industry which rapidly grew to employ many thousands of people on seven specific sites across the town, all of which were amalgamated into the Workington Iron and Steel Co. in 1909. This book chronicles the establishment and development of each of these original iron and steel works.

0 7524 3196 X

## Workington Association Football Club
PAUL EADE

This book contains over 200 images recording the history of the club. From the early days in the North Eastern League, it charts Workington's entry into the Football League in 1951, the twenty-six years spent there, and the Reds' fortunes since their return to non-League football in 1977.

0 7524 2818 7

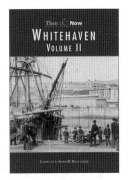

## Whitehaven Then & Now Volume II
ALAN ROUTLEDGE

This collection of over 85 pairs of images reveals some of the changes that have taken place in Whitehaven during the last century. Streets and buildings, organisations, shops and churches are shown as they used to be. Each pair is accompanied by informative text containing historical detail and local information sure to appeal to both the long established resident and the interested visitor.

0 7524 3094 7

## Cumberland Rugby League 100 Greats
ROBERT GATE

Cumberland had been producing great players since the Northern Union was founded in 1895. Coastal towns such as Whitehaven, Workington, Maryport and Millom have been major exports of skilful rugby players to the great clubs of Lancashire and Yorkshire, while fine exponents of the sport have issued from villages such as Seaton, Ellenborough, Broughton and Wath Brow. This book provides a detailed low-down on each player, and gives a taste of what it felt like to be on the touchline when these memorable men were in action.

0 7524 2731 8

If you are interested in purchasing other books published by Tempus, or in case you have difficulty finding any Tempus books in your local bookshop, you can also place orders directly through our website

www.tempus-publishing.com